ODE TO EL CAMINO DE SANTIAGO
and OTHER POEMS OF JOURNEY

ODE TO EL CAMINO DE SANTIAGO
and OTHER POEMS OF JOURNEY

JAMES E. GREEN

RESOURCE *Publications* · Eugene, Oregon

ODE TO EL CAMINO DE SANTIAGO
AND OTHER POEMS OF JOURNEY

Resource Publications
An Imprint of Wipf and Stock Publishers
199 W. 8th Ave., Suite 3
Eugene, OR 97401

www.wipfandstock.com

PAPERBACK ISBN: 978-1-6667-3600-7
HARDCOVER ISBN: 978-1-6667-9376-5
EBOOK ISBN: 978-1-6667-9377-2

JANUARY 7, 2022 10:54 AM

Contents

Acknowledgments

I WOULD LIKE TO THANK *Flying Island* for nominating "Summer Solstice on the West Coast of Ireland" for *Best of the Net* 2020. I also thank the Poetry Society of Indiana for recognizing several of these poems in contests it sponsored:

- "Ode to El Camino de Santiago" as the first prize winner in the Noble Poets Category in its 2020 contest;
- "Civil War in Myanmar" as second prize winner in the Wild Card category in its 2020 contest;
- "Tonight There are No Stars" as honorable mention in the Debra Sue Lynn Award category of its 2020 contest.

In addition, I thank Poets and Patrons, Inc., for recognizing the following poems in contests it sponsored;

- "Flight," as first place prize winner in the Nature category of its 2021 contest;
- "Morning on Soi Charoen Krung 85, Near Wat Worachan-yawas, Bangkok" as second place prize winner in its 2021 contest.

I also thank the following publications for previously publishing some of the poems in this collection:

- "I Look for a Pizza Menu and Find the Dharma of Buddha Instead, *Last Stanza Poetry Journal* (Winter, 2022)

- "Look Homeward, Angel," *Last Stanza Poetry Journal* (Summer, 2021)

- "The Weight of the Heart," *Flying Island* (February, 2021)

- "Bridge over River Kwai," *Last Stanza Poetry Journal* (Winter, 2021)

- "Okefenokee," "In the High Sierras," and "Tonight There Are No Stars" in *Grand Little Things* (February, 2021)

- "Civil War in Myanmar," in *Ink to Paper, Vol. 5* (Winter, 2020)

- "Summer Solstice on the West Coast of Ireland," *Flying Island* (June 2020)

- "Ode to El Camino de Santiago," *Valyermo Chronicle* (Fall 2020)

- "All Portals to the Past," *Last Stanza Poetry Journal* (Summer, 2020)

- "Preparing Gifts," *Last Stanza Poetry Journal* (Summer, 2020)

- "The Silo," *Poetry Midwest* (August, 2007)

Further, I gratefully acknowledge those poets whose work inspired several poems in this collection. In particular, "Summer Solstice on the West Coast of Ireland" was inspired by Seamus Heaney's "Postscript," "Preparing Gifts" was inspired by Seamus Heaney's "Clearances," "Ode to El Camino de Santiago" was inspired by C.P. Cavafy's "Ithaka," "Flight" was inspired by Eric Nelson's "Herons," and "I Look for a Pizza Menu and Find the Dharma of Buddha Instead' was inspired by Francis Gaspar's "Dog Days." The title and two of the lines in "Look Homeward, Angel," of course, belong to Thomas Wolfe.

ODE TO EL CAMINO DE SANTIAGO

To find *El Camino de Santiago*
begin wherever light and shadow mingle,
wherever questions stubbornly stay tangled
in threads of worn-out pieties and the soul

speaks to a longing for discovery
of the pilgrim's way, points the heart's compass
toward healing and offers silent witness
to that part of you that is solitary.

El Camino de Santiago is long,
though do not count the miles nor should you hurry;
Let time be measured by the way an early
morning mist arrives, dissolves, is gone.

And do not fear the way: There are no ghosts
to haunt (except your own), no Charybdis
and Scylla force the choice between abyss
or certain wreckage on a craggy coast

unless you have chosen to keep them deep
inside your soul. Leave them behind then feel
the sun warm the nape of your neck, smell
the fresh cut hay drying in the fields, keep

your eyes on the horizon and your mind
at rest, your heart open to new visions –
a new understanding – of destination,
of arrival, and along the way find

those sacred spaces where clarity
comes not from tortured thought but alights
as a winged peace in the quiet of night
or in the still shade of an olive tree.

Finally, when you make Compostela
and reach to touch the face of Santiago
worn smooth by all those before you, know
that what you tried to grasp along the way

now has hold of you.

Look Homeward, Angel

Although I'm told *you can't go home again*
the logic failed at the sound of a crow's rasping caw

echoing through a portal of leafless tress pressed
against the leaden sky of a winter morning,

swallowing lost time, summoning things past
and once again I am walking at dawn

from a pasture to the milking barn, feeling
the crunch of frozen grass at footfall,

hearing the pulse of machines steady as a heartbeat,
the clangor of metal chutes opening and closing

as Holsteins bump in and out of order,
barely overcoming their inertia while they

stare obliviously with pure black eyes so large
they hold my reflection, a reflection that says

look homeward, angel,

the sentiment too genuine for mere theory
and summoning cellular memory

of retreats into the solitude of the barn loft
and the fragrance of alfalfa hay and sight

of its dust floating in a shaft of slanted light
shining through chinks in the side of the barn

and I reach to touch one more time
the burnished handle of a hay hook

hanging on a wall with a tangle of binder-twine,
thin coarse slack-twists of sisal someone

thought to save as probably useful,
then forgot.

Summer Solstice on the West Coast of Ireland

This afternoon the sun is more a rumor,
probably still high behind a stretch
of somber clouds in shades of dappled grey.
The wind is brisk and plumes of ocean spray
rise against the cliffs and sea foam drifts
all the way to the bog, settles on the stubble
of freshly cut hay and backs of sheep that face
to lee, huddled against the day marked
as the longest since the age of hoary-haired men
dressed in ragged wool capes who aligned
boulders to measure their place in creation,
who tuned their lives to follow the light
like the lilies on the bank of the estuary.
It's why I've come here, a blow-in like
the neckless starlings motionless on the wire.
Sometimes they fly to a standstill against the wind
before suddenly rising as one winged flight
into an updraft, turning with the precision
of a drill team, becoming specks then disappearing.
Yes, it's why I've come here. I come here
to be neither here nor there, to be in a place
where strange is familiar, where it is normal
on summer solstice to light a turf fire,
its fragrance taking hold of you.

The Weight of the Heart

Consider the physics of the heart:
Pressure and volume in quarter note measure,
systoles and diastoles obedient to natural order,
electrified ebb and flood through chambers,

impulses igniting neurons surging, resting,
liquifying breath billions of times in a lifetime
transferring energy (we are told) like a universe,
like the history of time in miniature.

Consider the weight of the heart:
Less than a pound, though considerably more
when aching, incalculable at the point of breaking,
thus known for its infinite elasticity allowing it

to harbor sorrows that swell with time
or play host to spores of rancor that propagate
like mold in the recesses of a space before
turning to dark ravenous masses,

explaining why the Egyptians believed
in afterlife a heart was weighed against
a feather, and those souls with hearts heavier
were given to *Ammit* to be devoured

and hearts lighter were admitted into
the eternal bliss of the *Fields of Aʾaru*;
The Egyptians understanding (it seems)
what weighs the heart.

Tonight There Are No Stars

Tonight there are no stars, there is no sky,
only yellow smudges from streetlights glow
like ghost eyes from inside the fog that lies
heavy laden like a melting cloud low
to the ground while gauzy silhouettes appear,
fade, vanish, regather themselves in a hush
like phantasms hovering in mutable air
beyond the scope of sound or realm of touch.
It's why I like to walk alone on nights
like this: The edges soften, silence speaks,
opaqueness mutes what stirs disquiet, lights
awakening, as low-anchored mist leaks
onto my skin, into my pores, and thought
dissolves into a presence stillness brought.

The Bridge over River Kwai

Tourists pose at the Bridge over River Kwai,
while long-tail boats lazily glide
into berths beside floating restaurants –
signs for phat thai and Pepsi 100 bhat.

On the other side of the river, where
the rails reach vanishing point, a four-story
Buddha poses in meditation as though
listening for, hearing, echoes across

a span of time, sounds of prisoners straining
under the weight of timbers, hammering rails
into place, shouts of guards bludgeoning those
who collapse in exhaustion. I listen too:

It's the battalion whistling that song
as they march smartly across their new bridge
moments before it is bombed to rubble
and the water turns to fire.

There must be a lesson here: Something called
Death Railway featured in a guide book titled
Lonely Planet, a colossal concrete
Buddha meant, I suppose, to reverence

the site where POW's, all from
Christian nations a world away and who
died by legions alongside conscripted
Thai and Burmese, also buried by legions,

where sunlight falls through the gaps between
the bridge's wooden planks, and in shadows
floating on the water's surface faces
appear, disappear, then reappear

in a river that flows with a memory
of evil, and this tune from a movie
that keeps playing in my head
in present perfect tense.

Morning on Soi Charoen Krung 85, near Wat Worachanyawas, Bangkok

Fumes from a *songthaew* easing through the maze
of motorbikes and pushcarts rise visibly
into haze that begins to collect and tint the sun
a deeper, warmer hue of saffron, the same

as robes of monks collecting alms as they glide
along the fringe of the street past bins
with fresh vegetables and melons, cauldrons
with boiling peanuts, and fish packed in ice.

A monk stops where an old woman stirs curry
simmering over a brazier, the aroma mingling
with the scent of lotus blossoms rising
from a smear of algae in a shallow canal nearby.

Smiling, with folded hands touching her eyebrows,
she bows while he chants a blessing, its rhythm
and rising pitch telling me this is no ordinary
benediction given as trade for breakfast; no,

something is being turned loose, something
beyond the scope of words or reach of senses
except the one I cannot name but brings
an instant of palpable stillness to the particle

of space where they stand, as though someone
muted the sound for what might have been a movie
called *Soi 85 in the Morning* while the scenes' extras
pass by, moving in and out of focus.

A cat strays by, raises its tail while brushing against
the monk's robe and a taxi pulls-up, the driver gathering
what I guess to be a standing order for his lunch.
Next door a machine shop opens for business.

ON SPOTTING A PEBBLE OF QUARTZ
AT BAYON, ANGOR THOM

Tourists elbow their way up the stairway
leading to Vishnu who stares in all directions.
Halfway up they stop to pose for selfies
in front of Naga whose serpentine heads
fan out behind them. Other gods and goddesses
and Buddhas in bas-relief follow my progress
through the corridors, under and over archways
all scribed with visions of the cosmos
in all its fertility, in all the human form's
tenuous hold on inevitability.

On a terrace away from the crowd
in the company of another looming deity,
I spot a pebble of quartz on the ground
at the foot of an elephant guarding an alcove –
the perfect souvenir – a droplet of earth,
formed layer by crystalline layer, translucent
when I hold it to the light and I see inside
sparks of its creation, holding it this way
then that way, and I hear myself think,
or maybe something else say, *leave it*,
so I set it back.

Outside the temple walls,
where my tuk-tuk driver lounges
under a banyan tree,
I buy a postcard from a girl about ten,
her eyes the clearest I have ever seen.

Afternoon in Marrakech

Sunlight seeps through haze the afternoon
has collected, sinks onto canvas awnings

of *souks* at the edge of *Djemaa el-Fnaa*,
slips through tiny rents and casts

specks of light onto shadows
where women in hajibs, some in burkas,

sort produce into flat baskets, their fluid chatter
untethered to the work of hands.

A knot of men spills from a mosque then scatters,
some to the *souks*, a few to a *maqhaa* to games

of backgammon, the pieces all still in place,
and others disappear into a swarm of motorbikes.

A feral cat dodges a Vespa, raises its back and
struts to safety, curls around a post then

plops onto a spot of shade, flipping its tail
at anyone who noticed its brief loss of insouciance.

How familiar it feels to be the stranger,
to know the consolation of aloneness in a place

both alien and native, to see heat rise from cobblestones,
feel scorching air sink deep inside the lungs, and listen

to silent echoes of the call to prayer.

IN THE HIGH SIERRAS

When climbing in the High Sierras you learn
that timber lines are more or less approximate:
Branches start to sag like the shoulders of old men
in sparse patches of pines stooped from the weight
of winter snow, though now bare from summer's heat,
where the forest thins and turns to chaparral
then to slabs of craggy granite that emit
occasional glints from specks of embedded crystal.
Summit in sight, first you notice the shadow
attached at your soles, growing longer as the sun
scribes an arc to the horizon, then begins to show
that blush-colored measure of time that comes
at the fringe of the day and says to find
some shelter for the night and from the wind.

THE OKEFENOKEE

Eight o'clock: Already the heat chokes.
Swarms of gnats hover over the slough.
A gator prowling beneath the surface pokes,
then slides along, the keel of the canoe

while a great blue, motionless, poses on a log
half-submerged in water the color of tea.
It unfurls its wings and launches with one tug,
rising to the mossy crown of a cypress tree.

A crew of quarreling sparrows takes flight.
An otter scurries for shelter beneath a mangrove.
A sandhill crane lets loose a rattling cry,
full-throated, primal, as the swamp begins to move.

I cannot see nor hear what it might fear;
although, it must be near.

FLIGHT

Looking for still waters
the psalmist recommends,

I like to walk beside a small lake
that strays through farmland,

water shallow enough that stumps
poke through the surface and

the water's edge leaks into sloughs
hidden in the shade of sycamores

where often I will spot a heron
perched on one leg, alert as a sentry

and still as the air, its blue-gray
palette the work of an artist.

That's when I try to close-in,
slowly, quietly, without stealth,

and just as it seems the heron
is allowing me, trusts me,

it unfolds those glorious wings
and pulls itself into flight,

muscle and cartilage straining
against the burden of gravity,

legs dangling inches above the water,
as it glides to the other side,

alights, re-folds its wings
and resumes its pose, reproving me

to stay my distance.

Preparing Gifts

No one was home but us and now I know
she meant to make the utmost of her time.
Some gifts were scattered on the kitchen bench
and she asked if I would like to lend a hand.

She smoothed a leaf of foil then began
to show me how positioning just so
aligns the pattern at the fold, to trim
the ends so mitered corners matched. Such care.

Rough hands from housework and chores at the barn
when help was scarce delicately pressed the seams
while I laid over and tied the ribbon.
All that was long ago, though I remember.

I remembered as the nurse eyed the dials,
measured the drip through the needle puncturing
the back of her hand, skin aged thin as the tissue
we used for pre-wrapping what was fragile,

Remembering the two of us preparing gifts.
Never feeling closer.

All Portals to the Past Stay Open Wide

All portals to the past stay open wide,
although we know the passage is one-way.
We seek to have again what time abides.

Across the threshold to the other side
of thought, in shadowlands, where we assay
all portals to the past that open wide

acquaintances, friends, mentors, lovers cry
and laugh, in silence speak while echoes say
to seek, to hear again, what time abides.

A phrase forgotten raptures, a sound collides
inside the fault-line of a memory,
when portals to the past are open wide.

A snapshot tucked inside a book confides.
Old letters bound in string ignite lost days.
We seek to touch again what time abides.

You can't go home again, I've heard it said.
Although we try, the passage is one-way.
All portals to the past stay open wide.
We seek to have again what time abides.

The Silo

Inside the silo my echo rose to the opening
in the sky arousing memories of summer days

and the same urge to climb as in those years ago
so I reached for the first rung, a lead pipe worn slick

by the boots of men and bare feet of boys,
the ends buried deep in concrete hardened by years.

The first few rungs are wider apart, a span some builder
must have thought a child could not stretch the distance.

Of course, we did, and the higher you go
the rungs grow closer and climbing becomes easier:

hand on rung, foot on rung, hand again, foot again,
toward a circle of absolute blue, higher then higher

to where the span between the rungs and years disappears
and the circle begins to scribe a wider sky, until the top,

where I stand waist to head above the rim with the same
lump in my throat, remembering the first time

white knuckled fear gathered deep in my belly
as I looked over the edge onto the sea of fields.

CIVIL WAR IN MYANMAR

I *The Village*

For as long as memory this is home:
a circle of houses surrounding one for the altar,

vegetable patches on the fringe of the clearing,
opposite the side where our elephants lounge

at the end of their day, next to the path
that leads to the grove, and beyond it the river.

For as long as memory I hear the stories:
of tigers in the night, of heroes from old times,

of serpents and a savior from the new,
of places a world away and people a world apart,

of who to trust and of what to fear and where to hide,
stories to make us laugh and cry and wonder.

For as long as memory I see sunlight filtering
into our house through the wall of woven bamboo,

checkered patterns of white light creeping along the floor
as the sun falls, fading into the folds of mosquito netting

draped over a pallet in a corner where the baby sleeps,
shadows tiptoeing across the sky above the forest.

For as long as memory aromas linger:
of curry simmering while smoke from a fire

curls upward, rising like the blessings we give,
of fresh rain rinsing leaves of grass in the fields,

purifying the trees where we pick ripe fruit,
scents seeping into skin as water soaks the earth.

For as long as memory I feel the heartbeat
of my mother as I lay on her breast as she cradles me;

I feel the elephant's coarse hide beneath my thighs,
the hands of my father guiding mine when planting,

my soles sinking into the moist red earth, all
for as long as memory.

II   *Flight*

The origin of flight is fear.
We cannot choose to stay

at home if home is soon to be
the muzzles of their guns

or sounds of soldiers laughing while
our daughters scream, then sob.

The scout had said we had two days.
Our council met, we packed,

we met to pray our rosary,
in haste we ate, we fled.

The homes we built that soon we knew
would be in flames, then ashes,

the harvest we would never see
weighed heavy on our hearts,

a silent grief as palpable,
as odorous, as death.

I thought of Lot and how he warned
his wife to not look back.

Although, I did, with hope the salt
might cauterize my wounds;

Instead they bled.

We cannot choose to stay at home
if home is soon to be

thatched roofs turned into plumes of flames,
the muzzles of their guns,

the sounds of soldiers laughing while
our daughters scream, then sob.

One's flight from home is born of fear
while knowing that one step,

one footfall on a shaded path,
might find a landmine from

your father's war – a risk you take
when leaving home behind.

III *IDP Camp Near Myitkyina*

We have no measure of time
in a place that that is not our home,

a place where our flesh is not of the dirt,
where our bones are not of the trees.

Here the sun shines,
but leaves no halo over my daughter's face,

no longer warms the nape of my neck
nor kisses the dragon fruit on the trees.

There are no trees, and my daughter left;
she said to find work in the city.

My son, also. They escape from exhausted hope
into the jaws of the tiger.

Only women who nurse babies remain,
along with children who roam alleys

empty of laughter and old women
with dull eyes who sit alone in corners,

whose men stand in lines – one for bottled water
another for food vouchers – or sit on stoops.

There are no gardens for weeding, only weeds,
there are no chickens pecking at seeds scattered in yards,

only silent regrets hiding in the corridors of memory,
stirring awake hearts buried far from home,

hanging on to the few threads connecting
ghost-cries to prayer, faith to hope.

I Look for a Pizza Menu and Find the Dharma of Buddha Instead

Heading south on I-75
somewhere between Calhoun and Kennesaw,
I pull into a cheap motel for the night.
The sort of place where you find
a wide selection of porn for rent on the TV
and a Gideon's Bible on the nightstand.

After a hot shower I look for a pizza delivery menu.
None in sight. I try the drawer to the nightstand.
No menu. No Gideon's. Instead
is a book called *The Dharma of Buddha.*

I am ignorant about many things,
a condition I now accept as chronic,
but I have heard about *karma,*
so I begin reading – only pages on the left side,
the ones in English. On the right are rows
of symbols sketched in precise, delicate strokes.
Not Chinese, because I heard they write vertically,
the way some poets do. Either way,
I accept on faith the right side
means the same as the left,
and I start dog-earing pages –
a chapter on *Causation,*
another for *The Middle Way,*
which sounds a lot like Aristotle.
A coincidence, maybe.
Or, the Hand of Providence.
I cannot know these things.
For future reference I flag a chapter on
The Search for Truth.
Another on *Impermanence and Egolessness.*

Vanity of vanities, all things are vanity . . .
all rivers go to the sea, sayeth Qoheleth.
How far did the prophets, the ones of the Levant,
travel in their caravans? To what lands
did the stars they followed lead them?
What did they learn?
The magi who came from far away in the east,
how far to the east was their origin?

The index intrigues me most.
Page number and line for
five things no one can accomplish in this world.
And where to find *four states of unlimited mind.*
Under the heading *Mental Training* is a fable:

how one will find teachings for human life
wherever one goes.

WHERE HOME WAS

A tangle of ivy I cannot remember climbs
haphazardly to my room's window sill,
clings to field-rock walls by tiny tendrils
and forms a mesh of boney branches binding

time to place. Trace these vines to the ground
and you will find they have thick gnarled roots
as big as fists. A face I know looks
from the window clouded by years to a pond

where a boy fishes, to a grove of post oaks
where he builds his fort, but now where fences
sag and a Farmall tractor's carcass rusts,
where snows have fallen, melted, soaked

into the earth, into the loamy red clay.
Be still. You will hear it whisper my name.

JAMES GREEN

JAMES has worked as a naval officer, deputy sheriff, high school English teacher, professor of education, and administrator in both public schools and universities. His academic publications include three books, as well as numerous monographs and articles in professional journals. Recipient of two Fulbright grants, he served as a visiting scholar at the University of Limerick in Ireland and the National Chung Cheng University in Taiwan. He has published four chapbooks of poetry in addition to this collection, and individual poems have appeared in literary magazines in England, Ireland, and the USA. James has received numerous awards for his poetry, among them the Charles Dickson Chapbook Prize sponsored by the Georgia Poetry Society for *Long Journey Home*. He also was nominated for Best of the Net for "Summer Solstice on the West Coast of Ireland," as well as for the MLA Conference on Christianity and Literature Book of the Year for *Stations of the Cross* (Finishing Line Press). He holds B.A. and M.S. degrees in English and Education from Missouri State University, a Ph.D. in Education from Saint Louis University, and an M.F.A. in Creative Writing from Antioch University Los Angeles.

You can learn more about James' poetry through his website at **www.jamesgreenpoetry.net.**

www.ingramcontent.com/pod-product-compliance
Lightning Source LLC
Chambersburg PA
CBHW071801020426
42331CB00008B/2353